MAKING THE MOST OF

YOUR CHILD'S TEACHABLE MOMENTS

MAKING THE MOST OF

YOUR CHILD'S TEACHABLE MOMENTS

Wanda B. Pelfrey

MOODY PRESS

CHICAGO

© 1988 by
THE MOODY BIBLE INSTITUTE
OF CHICAGO

All Scripture quotations, unless noted otherwise, are from the King James Version.

Library of Congress Cataloging in Publication Data

Pelfrey, Wanda B.
    Your child's teachable moments / by Wanda B. Pelfrey.
       p.   cm.
    ISBN 0-8024-5205-1
    1. Christian education of children.   2. Children—Religious life.
  3. Children—Conduct of life.   I. Title.
    BV1475.2P45   1988
248.8'4—dc19   88-12917
                                    CIP

3 4 5 6 7 8 Printing/DP/Year 93 92 91 90 89

Printed in the United States of America

Contents

Teach Them to Your Children   7

Teachable Moments at Home
1. Getting Up   10
2. Going to Bed   12
3. When Your Child Wants to Help   15
4. Oops   17
5. Making Yeast Bread   19
6. Breaking Something   21
7. Grandparents   23
8. Being a Neighbor   25
9. Sick in Bed   28
10. Company Comes   31

Teachable Moments Away from Home
11. Waiting   36
12. Going to Church   38
13. A Trip to the Grocery Store   40
14. A Trip to the Mall   42
15. Going to a Ball Game   45
16. Going to the Zoo   47
17. Going on a Trip   49

Teachable Moments in Nature

18. A Big Storm   54
19. Seeing a Rainbow   56
20. Seeing Mountains   59
21. Seeing the Ocean   61

Teachable Moments During Seasons

22. Spring   66
23. Summer   68
24. Changing Leaves   70
25. First Snowfall   73

Teachable Moments During Holidays and Celebrations

26. Easter   78
27. Mother's Day / Father's Day   80
28. The Fourth of July   82
29. Halloween   84
30. Thanksgiving   87
31. Cutting or Buying the Family Christmas Tree   89
32. Family Birthdays   91

Teachable Moments in New Experiences

33. The First Day of School   96
34. First Overnighter   99
35. Moving to a New Town   101
36. Arrival of a New Brother or Sister   104
37. Moving to a New Home   107
38. Going to the Hospital   110

Teachable Moments in Sadness

39. The Cat Disappears   116
40. The Death of a Pet   119
41. A Death in the Family   122

Teach Them to Your Children

Like most passages of Scripture that flow soothingly off our tongues, Deuteronomy 11:19 stands out for another reason: it is downright practical.

God knew way back when the book of Deuteronomy was written that we would spend more time with our children in routine activities than we would in formal worship activities at church or at home.

God also never intended our worship of Him to be limited to formal activities of worship. Being a child of God should influence how we shop, how we do our jobs, how we keep house, how we play.

When this is true of you as a parent, the natural result is to teach your child the truths of God's Word by "talking about them when you sit at home and when you walk along the road, when you lie down and when you get up" (NIV*).

This book is meant to help you include God as a regular participant in your everyday life. He is always there. We only need to remember to recognize His presence.

*New International Version.

TEACHABLE MOMENTS AT HOME

1

Getting Up

How a person views getting out of bed in the morning is an individual matter. In fact, you may have several differing opinions in your own family. Greeting each day with thanksgiving and expectancy can be gently cultivated in your child.

ACTIVITY STARTERS

1. Depending on the temperament of your child, wake him in a gentle or lively manner by singing Psalm 118:24 to the tune "London Bridge."

> This is the day the Lord has made,
> The Lord has made,
> The Lord has made,
> This is the day the Lord has made,
> Let us rejoice and be glad in it.

2. Again using Psalm 118:24, greet your child as he comes to breakfast with, "This is the day which the Lord hath

made." Teach him to respond by saying, "We will rejoice and be glad in it."

3. After praying for God's guidance for the day, ask, "What do you want to do with this new day?" Be prepared to relate your own goals to him.

4. For several days go through a step-by-step prayer of thanks with your child. As you wake him up pray, "Thank You, God, for the warm, safe night." As your child washes up pray, "Thank You, God, for clean water to use." As he selects his clothes pray, "Thank You, God, for providing these good, warm (or comfortable) clothes." After a few mornings, your child should be able to begin his days thanking God without your help.

5. After your child is in bed, occasionally slip into his room and post happy notes. "I love you," "You are special," and "God loves you" are all messages that will help bring an early morning smile even if he has to wait for someone to read them to him. Nonverbal notes could include a smiling face or heart drawn with a colorful marker.

A BIBLE VERSE TO TALK ABOUT

"Walk in wisdom toward them that are without, redeeming the time" (Colossians 4:5). God's Book says we should see every day as a new opportunity to tell someone about Christ. We should look for opportunities to be kind and helpful.

2

Going to Bed

Learning Opportunity

Some children tolerate going to bed better than others. From her earliest days, my youngest daughter considered the time scheduled for sleep totally wasted. Only now, as she approaches her teen years, does she view it more favorably. However your child views bedtime, your goal should be to make it a pleasant time when he is aware of God's care.

Activity Starters

1. Establish a time for bed and a bedtime routine. You will have to be flexible. If you live in a family where everyone is at home just before bedtime, you may want to have a time of family Bible reading and prayer. Enjoy these days, as schedules become more complicated as children grow older. If it is not possible to have devotions as a family, a separate time of Bible stories and prayer for each child may still be possible. If your child falls asleep during the middle of supper each night, assume he is a morning person, and consider the suggestions in the previous chapter. The important thing is that bedtime be pleasant and

structured around your family's needs, not a schedule from a book. Spend time as a family talking about what makes the best bedtime.

2. Help your child evaluate his day. Along with, "Have you brushed your teeth and fed the gerbil?" you might ask, "What did you do today that you think pleased God the most?" Perhaps your child could keep a picture diary. Provide a notebook and crayons by his bedside for him to draw a quick picture of the event. Your questions may produce a negative confession, but a guilty conscience does not allow even a preschooler to sleep well.

3. If your child always seems wide awake at bedtime, use the time for talking or reading together. You can probably read books a little beyond your child's age level. Books read together will often be reread by the child when he is older. Choose books that cover subjects your child needs to be aware of or that will lead to conversations on those subjects. Christian fiction for children often deals with vital issues.

4. Accept your child as an individual. If he is fretful or fearful at bedtime, treat his concerns seriously, and do your best to respond to them. You might say, "What you are worried about does not worry me, but it is important to me to help you feel better. When something is bothering me, I do two things. I see what the Bible says about it, and I pray."

5. Buy a supply of Bible story tapes or Christian music tapes (also check your public or church library). Young children can learn to operate tape players, and the tapes can be a source of soothing enrichment as the child falls asleep. You might say, "Christian music helps me feel better. I think it will help you rest better, because it will help you think of God and His love."

A Bible Verse to Talk About

"I will both lay me down in peace, and sleep: for thou, Lord, only makest me dwell in safety" (Psalm 4:8). God's Book says God is always watching over us. It is good to go to sleep and know that God never sleeps.

3

When Your Child Wants to Help

I never have seen a study proving that children who are allowed to help when they are young will retain that trait when they reach their teenage years. Their desire to help seems to vanish with the arrival of their ability to help. Since their desire is short-lived, it should be nurtured and used as an opportunity to teach—even though most tasks are easier to do by yourself.

ACTIVITY STARTERS

1. Explain your work ethic to your child. Do you feel speed, quality, or neatness is the most important? You might say, "The Bible tells us in Colossians 3:23 that everything we do should be done as if we were doing it for God. If I am painting this fence to honor God, I should work as neatly as possible."
2. Take time to teach your child a skill, such as how to use a piece of sandpaper or how to wash dishes properly. He can practice that skill near you as you do the more detailed work. We often underestimate children's abilities to

master useful skills as they are playing. Talk about things Joseph might have taught Jesus in the carpentry shop. Ask, "Do you think Jesus was a careful worker?"

3. Allow your child to help you work for the Lord and His church. He can help sort food for a benevolent work, accompany you as you canvas a neighborhood, help clean a classroom, or do many other tasks. Treat him as a coworker for the Lord, not as a child to be kept out from underfoot.

4. Cherish work time as an opportunity to talk with your child. People seem to talk more easily when they are working together than if they just sit down to talk. Keep a mental file of subjects you need to talk about. Be sensitive to any subject he brings up. These opportunities become more rare and precious as children grow older. Treasure them now for their true worth.

5. Praise effort, not outcome. If something does not turn out right, remind your child that he was trying to be helpful. Talk about what went wrong. Help him plan how to do it better the next time, and then help repair any damage. Recount the first time you tried to do something for the Lord that you now do well, such as sing a solo or teach a class. Most of us have improved over our first attempts. Ask him if he thinks God is pleased that you tried again.

A Bible Verse to Talk About

"Whatsoever thy hand findeth to do, do it with thy might" (Ecclesiastes 9:10). God's Book teaches us that we should keep busy doing useful things. If we do our best, we will usually enjoy what we do.

4
Oops

Childhood carries with it the burden of messy accidents. These can range from spilling a small glass of juice to the "accidental" pouring of a package of sugary gelatin onto a newly waxed floor. (My youngest daughter and I survived both of these and many more.) Most of these can be classified as everyday nuisances, but since we experience more of this type of mishap during our lives than major catastrophes, we should consider the effect they have on our children.

ACTIVITY STARTERS

1. In a first-aid class for child care workers, I was told, "Treat the child before you treat the injury." The same would be true when a child makes a big mess. Be sure to communicate to him that he is more important than a clean kitchen floor (or new carpet). Ask, "Which do you think God believes is more important, you or this floor?" Assure him that you also believe that he is more important.
2. Help him clean up the mess. As you work together tell him, "Often people have to ask God for help in their lives

17

like you needed my help to clean up this spill. God is always willing to help us when we ask Him."

3. To the tune of "This Is the Way We Wash Our Clothes" you can sing, "This is the way we mop up juice, mop up juice, mop up juice. This is the way we mop up juice on this Monday morning." Adapt the words to fit the accident and the day. Music can ease the strain of the moment. Continue the changed mood by singing songs about God's love.

4. Play "It Could Have Been Worse" with your child. Take turns naming ways his accident could have been worse. Don't worry if it becomes a little silly. When you have exhausted all possibilities, say, "People sometimes get upset about little things because they don't think about how big the problem could have been. God knows everything. Do you imagine God must think we are silly when we get upset about spilled juice?"

5. Help your child to speculate about accidents children in the Bible might have had. Did David ever drop his harp or trip over a lamb? Did Moses ever spill his juice in Pharaoh's palace? Did Jesus ever knock over a pile of wood in Joseph's carpentry shop? (The Bible tells us Jesus never sinned—not that He did not have the same accidents as other children.) Not only will such speculation help your child put his accident into perspective, but it will enable him to relate to Bible people as real.

A BIBLE VERSE TO TALK ABOUT

"We know that all things work together for good to them that love God" (Romans 8:28). God's Book promises us that God can use everything that happens to us to make us better. How do you think He can use spilling juice (or whatever) to make you and me better?

5
Making Yeast Bread

LEARNING OPPORTUNITY

Through the years, kneading bread has helped many women work out frustrations and worries. There are other good reasons for at least occasionally baking bread at home. One of the best is that it gives you the opportunity to introduce your children to the concept of patience.

ACTIVITY STARTERS

1. Follow a yeast bread recipe, and allow your child to help mix the dough. Pinch off a small amount, setting aside the remainder to rise. Help your child bake the smaller amount immediately. After the larger loaf has risen and has been baked, compare the two. Say, "Do you think the bigger loaf was worth waiting for? Often God has us wait for answers to our prayers. We must trust Him to know best."
2. Use the time the dough is rising to teach your child a new skill (for example, sewing, carpentry, or throwing a ball). If he becomes frustrated with his first efforts, remind him that God made people a lot like bread dough. It takes time

for a person to develop skills so that he can be more useful to himself, others, and God.

3. Teach your child that developing talents also takes time.
As you are mixing the dough, play Christian music in the
background. Ask your child if he thinks that the musician
sang or played that well the first time he tried. Tell him
that every good musician must work patiently for years to
develop the talent God gave him. You might say, "God
made yeast, but people must give it time to do its work."

4. Divide the yeast dough into small loaves before baking.
After they are baked and cooled, wrap them attractively,
and, along with your child, deliver them to neighbors or
shut-ins. After doing that ask, "Do you think that flour,
yeast, and sugar would have been appreciated as much if
we had delivered them before we mixed them together, or
before we let them rise, or before we baked them?" Your
child probably will think those ideas are funny. Then say,
"Sometimes we get impatient and want to do great things
before we are ready. We have to learn to trust God's timing."

5. If you don't want to bake, try to arrange a visit to a local
bakery. Ask someone there if the bread has to be given
time to rise. Your child will be more familiar with their
finished product. Remind him that even the modern bak-
er has to wait for the yeast to rise just as people in Bible
times did. Say, "Sometimes we only learn patience by being forced to wait."

A BIBLE VERSE TO TALK ABOUT

"Be still, and know that I am God" (Psalm 46:10). Many
people believe that being busy is the only good use of time.
We often rush to do things before we are ready. God's Book
tells us that everyone needs quiet times to patiently learn
more about Him.

6

Breaking Something

LEARNING OPPORTUNITY

Raising children is often detrimental to household items. Although we as parents value our children more than our possessions, occasionally an accident will upset us. When such an incident occurs, it is good to impress upon your child a vital truth from God's Word.

ACTIVITY STARTERS

1. Before you do anything else, accept your child's apology and offer your forgiveness. Pray with your child, "Dear God, as we look at this broken _____, we remember that only You and what is Yours lasts forever."

2. As you clean away the remains of the broken item (let the child help unless he is likely to be hurt) say, "Things like this _____ get broken or too old to use. Can you name some things that will last forever?" Help your child to realize that only things such as love, kindness, and the souls God gave us will last. The younger your child, the more difficult it will be for him to understand an abstract idea; the broken item will be much more real

to him. Remember that you are planting seeds. Do not be disappointed if your child does not seem to fully understand what you are talking about. He will understand your attitude.

3. Look at a catalog. Say, "This toy (or appliance) is shiny and new now. Will it always look like this?" Help the child see that shiny, new things become old with use. They are only meant to last a short time. Only God can make something last forever.

4. Say, "Look around this room and tell me what you think is the most important thing in it." Help him realize that people are the most important.

5. Examine the broken item in light of the following questions: First, was it important to the home? Second, to whom did it belong? Third, was the child being careless when he broke it? (This question will be answered more objectively after a little time has passed and reassurance has been given.) Finally, what should be done about it? Possible solutions would include: (1) Apologize to whomever it belonged. (2) Help replace it. (It will benefit the child to contribute even a few cents toward replacement or to do some chores to earn some of the replacement money.) (3) Forget about it, and try to be more careful. (After all, great-grandmother's china vase cannot be replaced, but a lesson can be learned.) (4) Mend it.

A BIBLE VERSE TO TALK ABOUT

"For I am the Lord, I change not" (Malachi 3:6). Change, whether planned or accidental, often makes us feel unhappy. Although our lives are full of change, God's Book tells us that God and His ways do not change. Let us be thankful for the security that gives us.

7
Grandparents

Learning Opportunity

Grandparents are an everyday, right-next-door commodity for some children—and a rare luxury for others. Near or far away, they are irreplaceable in a child's life, and he should be guided in enjoying them.

Activity Starters

1. Research your family tree. My oldest daughter did this in elementary school and my youngest as a Girl Scout, but, with help, a preschooler could enjoy learning about Mommy and Daddy's mommies and daddies and their mommies and daddies. Why not gather as many photographs as possible and mount them in chronological order. As you do this, show your child how the Bible traces Jesus' family order in Matthew 1 and Luke 3. Say, "You have a little bit of all your relatives in you, and that makes you special."

2. Encourage grandparents to tell about what life was like in their childhood. We teach our children more about respect for older people by example than by lecture. If pos-

sible, take family history trips with grandparents. These may include trips to old houses, cemeteries, or other towns or states. Make notes about things you will want to be able to help your child recall in later years. Give thanks for these people who are willing to participate in your child's life.

3. Worship together whenever possible. Sitting near grandparents and even great-grandparents can give a child a feeling of the continuity of the faith and will bear witness to the importance of worship.

4. As a family, look for ways to add joy to the lives of grandparents. If you live nearby, it could be a leaf-raking or weed-pulling visit or a meal with your family bringing the food and doing the cleaning up. If several hundred miles separate you, it might involve surprise parties by mail, cards, "Happy Birthday" sung over the telephone, and other long-distance visiting. Encourage your child to do things for these special people. Say, "Being good to parents and grandparents pleases Jesus." Also, the relating of everyday activities is especially important to grandparents. For long-distance grandparents, keep records of special accomplishments and make phone calls when extra-special events occur. Invite nearby grandparents to attend preschool, kindergarten, or church programs in which your child will participate.

5. Make a family project of finding out about grandparents mentioned in the Bible. Talk about ways they might have taught their grandchildren.

A BIBLE VERSE TO TALK ABOUT

"Cast me not off in the time of old age; forsake me not when my strength faileth" (Psalm 71:9). In God's Book David asks God to remember and use him when he grows old. Grandparents and other older people can teach us a lot if we will listen.

8
Being a Neighbor

Most of us bemoan the loss of the sense of neighborhood in our communities, yet we seldom do anything about it. Although it is true that interdependence of past generations may never reappear, most of us could help improve the situation and teach our children how to be better neighbors.

ACTIVITY STARTERS

1. Tell the story of the Good Samaritan to your child and talk about who your neighbors are and how God would want you to treat them. Let your preschooler accompany you as you begin a get-to-know-your-neighbor campaign. Be the first to wave. Take baked goods to a new neighbor along with an invitation to attend church with you if they have not found a church home. Take Christmas (or Easter or Valentine) cookies to neighbors to create an opportunity to get to know them better. You might say to your child, "You know the Good Samaritan took time to help the hurt man. I believe God wants us to take time to be good neighbors."

2. Be a peacemaker in your neighborhood. Refuse to gossip about a neighbor and explain why to your preschooler. Encourage your child to be considerate of neighbors' property and privacy. Set an example of keeping your yard and home neat so it is an asset to the neighborhood. Tell your preschooler, "God likes for us to think of others in all that we do."

3. By our actions as well as our words, we can teach our children that being a good neighbor does not necessarily mean approval of life-style. In our society, Christians often find themselves living next door to people who are openly disregarding God's laws. We may have to say, "No, you may not go to _____'s house, but you are to be kind and polite." By witnessing our kindness and helpfulness to such neighbors, our children will learn how to handle such situations. A smile, wave, or helping hand will not compromise our beliefs.

4. Be willing to host the neighborhood children. It helps to remember that this stage of your life will last for only a few years. When the children are playing in your yard or in your house, you will have the opportunity to influence them with Christian values. A private, kind statement such as, "We do not use words in this house that we feel Jesus would not like," can have a lasting influence on a child. Your loving acceptance of your child's friends will mean a lot to him.

5. Explain to your child what Jesus teaches in Matthew 25:31-45. Help him to understand that kindnesses done for those in need are like kind deeds for Jesus. Let your child help you be a helpful neighbor. If there is a death or sickness in a household, offer food or what help you can. Preschoolers can help care for pets or gather the mail for vacationing neighbors. Collecting an elderly neighbor's mail or newspapers could be a daily project for a four year old.

Frequently remind your preschooler that you know God is pleased by his helpfulness.

A Bible Verse to Talk About

"Thou shalt love thy neighbour as thyself" (Mark 12:31). God's Book teaches us to care about the feelings and needs of everyone we meet. Since we often meet the people we live near, we should be kind to them.

9
Sick in Bed

With the decline of many childhood diseases, extended sick-in-bed times have decreased. Colds and flu still put a child down occasionally, however, and present parents with unexpected quiet time with their children.

ACTIVITY STARTERS

1. There is often more housework to be done when someone is sick, but be sure to spend time with your child. If it seems the time of confinement will last beyond a couple of days, establish a schedule (flexible, of course) so he will feel assured of your company at certain times. Use these times to comfort, entertain, or both, depending on how sick your child is. Sometimes he may just want to rest his head in your lap. At other times, reading or playing games may please him. Use these times to remind him of God's presence and care. You might say, "It is never fun to be sick, but we can enjoy being together while you are getting better. God can make good use of even the times when you do not feel well."

2. Use the time your child is sick to teach him how to care for the body God gave him. Talk about good health habits—especially washing hands. Talk about the ways God has made his body able to fight disease and the ways he himself can help these systems along. You might say, "We are usually more useful to God and others when we are healthy. We cannot always avoid becoming sick, but we can do our best."

3. Encourage your child to use the quiet time to observe God's creation. If possible, put him near a window and suggest things he can look for. Birds, weather, and changes in light can all be observed from inside. If no suitable window is available, set up a nature display with plants, shells, pinecones, or rocks and a magnifying glass. Discuss the beauty of the things God made during free moments. Say something like, "You know, most of the time we are so busy we just step on a rock and never take time to look at it. It's nice to have a chance to really look at some things God has made."

4. As your child recovers, plan ways he can entertain himself. Bible storybooks that come with tapes are well suited for this. A box of small toys put away for such a time is helpful. Quiet music is especially helpful when a child needs to rest. A box of odds and ends of cardboard and paper plus glue and scissors can provide entertainment. A child usually becomes more trying as he recovers—just as you are becoming exhausted. New interests keep everyone's feelings in check and prevent a loving child from developing into a tyrant. This is a good time for a review of the Golden Rule. Sickness makes most of us more self-centered. Your child may need to be guided gently into thinking of others again.

5. If a child is sick on a Sunday and must miss church along with his caretaker, plan a brief time of worship. A record

or tape player can provide music. Reading from the Bible and a Bible storybook will be meaningful. This time does not need to be long. It is important that we emphasize the value of worship. You might say, "I miss being able to worship in church this morning, but I am glad that God is able to receive the worship we can give Him here."

A Bible Verse to Talk About

"Casting all your care upon him; for he careth for you" (1 Peter 5:7). Sometimes when we do not feel well, we worry and grumble and complain. God's Book tells us that God is with us and is taking care of us.

10

Company Comes

LEARNING OPPORTUNITY

Except for the few families who live in homes equipped with extra bedrooms, bathrooms, and a paid staff, even the most welcome of guests require a few changes and sacrifices by all family members. Developing a good attitude about these changes and sacrifices is the beginning of hospitality.

ACTIVITY STARTERS

1. Hold an informal planning meeting for all family members (perhaps during an evening meal) as soon as you know company is coming. Taking into consideration everyone's work and school schedules, plan where your guests will sleep. Try to accept any offers of beds when it is reasonable; however, a six-foot three-inch, two-hundred-and-fifty pound guest will not fit into most children's bunks even if the owner is willing to make the sacrifice. If the visit is to be extended, discuss which normal family activities can include the guests and which might need to be changed. Most adult or teenage guests will not mind being left at the house alone occasionally while dentist ap-

pointments or music lessons are kept. Give thanks for the opportunity to share your home. Use the experience to tell your child about the Person we have living with us all the time—Jesus.

2. Allow your preschooler to help with room preparations. Whether your guest room is a separate room or a fold-away sofa, some special touches will be appreciated. While you put on clean sheets, your child can carry in guest towels, pick a rose, and place some interesting reading material where it will be easily found. Even if the fold-away sofa is right in the middle of your living area, plan with your child ways to provide at least a small degree of privacy for the guest. The longer the stay, the more important this is. You might say, "When someone is away from their home they often feel uncomfortable. We want to make our guest feel like he is a member of our family." Ask your child, "Do you think Jesus is comfortable living in our home?"

3. Tell your child something about the upcoming guest unless it is someone he knows well and sees often. This person may have been your college roommate for four years, but unless they have met before, he still is a stranger to your preschooler. Let your child in on the reasons this person is special to you so he can have a head start on learning to love him also. Ask him, "Who is the most important Person who lives with us?"

4. Find ways to include your child in kitchen preparations. This will add to his anticipation, make the waiting easier, and give you a way to include him in mealtime conversation. Saying, "Did you know that Missy iced the cake?" will explain why it looks the way it does as well as make Missy feel important. While you are working together, tell

your child about Mary and Martha who prepared food for Jesus and His helpers.

5. Volunteer to keep some of God's servants overnight when they are visiting your church. Having a missionary, musical guest, or visiting preacher in your home can be a rewarding experience for your entire family. Discuss with your child how it pleases Jesus to put up guests cheerfully. Your warm hospitality will be appreciated more by your guest than the elegantly decorated guest room you wish you had. Encourage your child to be present when you are talking to your guest.

A BIBLE VERSE TO TALK ABOUT

"Use hospitality one to another without grudging" (1 Peter 4:9). God's Book encourages us to share our homes with others. This is called hospitality.

TEACHABLE MOMENTS
AWAY FROM HOME

11
Waiting

A great deal of our time is spent waiting—waiting in doctors' offices, in bank lines, at commuter stations, in checkout lines, or even at home. When this time is being spent with a small child, its length can seem to triple unless we have planned to use it creatively.

ACTIVITY STARTERS

1. Engage your child in an interesting conversation. This can be done even while standing in a line. Look around you until you locate an interesting item. Ask questions such as: "Why do you think God made _____?" "How does that _____ make you feel?" Listen and respond with your own impressions.
2. Keep a pencil and blank index cards or pad of paper in your purse. These are wonderful entertainment for a restless child. You can also use them to teach shapes, letters, and numbers as your child grows older. Profitable use of the time with which God has blessed us is always a good lesson.

3. Keep a few simple Bible verses copied on index cards in your purse or car. Work on memorizing them in spare moments. Encourage your child to do this with you. Be sure to take the time to explain what the verse means.
4. Play simple thought/word games with your child. Say, "I see something God created that is green. Its parts hang down." (A plant in the doctor's office.) If your view is limited, switch to, "I am thinking about something God created that is . . ."
5. Together make up songs to fit your situation or to give thanks for something you see. (This is best done when you are waiting in your car or at home.) Take a simple tune such as a nursery rhyme or commercial and put new words to it. For example, to the tune "London Bridge" you might put the words, "God made <u>flowers</u>, yes He did, yes He did, yes He did. God made <u>flowers</u>, yes He did. I'm so thankful." The underlined word can be changed to fit your needs.

A BIBLE VERSE TO TALK ABOUT

"I will bless the Lord at all times" (Psalm 34:1). God's Book teaches us that time used thinking about ways God has blessed us is always profitable. We can look at the beautiful things He made. We can think of the wonderful people He has given us to love.

12

Going to Church

Getting a family to church on Sunday morning can at times be anything but a spiritual experience. Our goals should be for everyone in the family to arrive on time and in a mood conducive to worship.

Activity Starters

1. Make going to church on Sunday an anticipated event by preparing for it on Saturday. Have a set time (right after supper or before bed) when you gather everyone's church clothes. Cleaning shoes, brushing suits, and checking hems can set the tone of being ready for worship. The emphasis should always be on cleanliness, not fashion. Give thanks for God's provision of clothes.
2. Review last Sunday's lesson with your child or preview the one for the coming week. Many children receive some type of take-home paper. Reading these with your child will provide some of the repetition important to learning for the preschool child. It will also help him look forward to returning to class.

3. Establish a simple but nourishing Sunday morning breakfast tradition. Gear it to your family's needs. For example, if your household has only one bathroom, a buffet of cereal, fruit, and sweet rolls to which all but the very young can help themselves might be more practical than pancakes, for which everyone would need to sit down together. The tradition sets Sunday apart as special. Tell your child, "We like Sunday to be special because it is God's special day."

4. Put on background music during your preparations. Find a radio station or play tapes or records that will prepare your hearts for worship. Sing choruses on the way to church.

5. Avoid conflict between family members if possible. Many problems or criticisms can be discussed at a later time. If necessary, write yourself a note and post it where it will catch your attention after lunch. (Many issues will no longer be important by then.) If there is more than one child in your household, you will need to enlist their help. Say something like, "We do not worship well when we are upset with one another. Will you help by saying only kind, happy things on Sunday morning? We can talk about problems at another time."

A Bible Verse to Talk About

"I was glad when they said unto me, Let us go into the house of the Lord" (Psalm 122:1). David wrote in God's Word that he was glad when he was able to worship God. How do you feel when we are getting ready for church on Sunday? Do you feel happy?

13

A Trip to the Grocery Store

LEARNING OPPORTUNITY

From the time a child is able to sit alone in a shopping cart, going to the grocery store becomes an experience. Whether that experience will be good or bad depends on how well his little hands and his mind are occupied. Making this chore more enjoyable is desirable. Making it spiritually profitable might sound too good to be true, but it is not impossible. What can we teach our children as we shop for food?

ACTIVITY STARTERS

1. Before leaving home or before getting out of the car at the parking lot, talk to your child about the ways God provides. "We should be thankful that Daddy (or Mommy) is healthy and has a good job. Why don't we thank Him for that? 'Dear God, we know that You know our family needs good food. Thank You for providing this money to buy it. Help us to spend it wisely.'"

2. As you are putting your child in the grocery cart, explain this game to him. "You watch what I put in the grocery cart. When you know what it is, whisper, 'Thank You,

God, for _____.' You do not have to say it
out loud. God can hear you even in this busy store. If you
do not know what something is, you may ask me."
3. Another game to be played can be explained, "Watch what
I put in the grocery cart. When I choose something you
are thankful for, ask to hold it. If I choose something you
are more thankful for, you may trade. When we have finished our grocery shopping, let's see if you are holding
the one thing you are most thankful for." This activity
will work well with even two or more children; however,
you may need to buy more than one of a certain item.
4. Fasten a piece of construction paper to a clipboard or
cardboard and give it, along with a sandwich bag of gold
stars, to your child. Say, "The Bible says in Matthew 6:8
that our Father knows what we need before we ask Him.
God knows we need good, healthy food. He has blessed us
with the money to buy it. You watch as I put food in the
cart. When I put something in that you think is a healthy
food, stick a star on your paper. When we are finished we
will see how many healthy foods we bought."
5. After you arrive home, putting the groceries away can be
a time of praise. Using a familiar tune such as, "Row,
Row, Row Your Boat," sing your thanks to God for the
food that He has provided. "Thank You, God, for peas,
thank You, God, for peas. For this and all good gifts,
thank You, God, for peas."

A BIBLE VERSE TO TALK ABOUT

"Take no thought for your life, what ye shall eat, or what
ye shall drink" (Matthew 6:25). God's Book says that we
do not need to worry about having enough to eat or drink
because God will give us what we need. We should always
remember to thank Him for providing food for us.

14

A Trip to the Mall

The mall is a familiar part of many families' lives. It seems to have taken the place of the small-town main street in fulfilling many of our marketing and socializing needs. Use your time there as a growing experience for your child.

ACTIVITY STARTERS

1. Provide for your child's physical needs before leaving home. A child who has not used a stroller in months may need one in a mall. Because it is an enclosed area, we sometimes forget how far we must walk from one store to another. Carry a few crackers or cookies and a small can of juice instead of relying on expensive mall food to help revive a tired child. If you do not already know, check the location of rest rooms as soon as you arrive. Being in a new place often brings on a desire in a preschooler to tour the rest rooms, but we all know that when the need is real it is urgent. Planning beforehand to meet those physical needs can make the difference between a pleas-

ant and disastrous trip and says to your child, "I love and care about you."

2. Allow time for a trip to the pet store. My daughters are now twelve and sixteen, and we still visit the pet store almost every trip. So far we have bought nothing bigger than a gerbil, but we have had many enjoyable moments. You might say to your child, "A pet store is a lot like a small zoo. It is full of different types of animals that God made. Which one do you like best? Why do you think God decided to make _____?"

3. Practice smiling. In our efforts to protect our children from strangers, we often have succeeded in making them fearful and downright unfriendly. Teach your child that, while it might be dangerous to start a conversation with someone they do not know, a smile is a gift they can give to anyone. Try it yourself. It often brings pleasant results.

4. Take advantage of activities at your local mall that will interest your child. Viewing seasonal decorations can be fun. Often puppet shows, musical performances, and displays are offered. Enjoy the activities with your child. Talk about what he liked or did not like about what was presented. Remind him that the person who performed was blessed by God with that talent.

5. Occasionally let your child shop at the mall (or any store). Provide a small amount of money, unless he has received some from another source. This will give you an opportunity to teach about the proper use of money. Say, "The Bible tells us that part of all the money we receive should be returned to God. Do you think that part should be put away first so you do not forget and spend it?" Then discuss such things as the careful use of money. In the end, let your child have the final decision about how he is going to spend his money. More lessons have probably been learned from bad purchases than from wise ones.

A Bible Verse to Talk About

"For God so loved the world, that he gave his only begotten Son" (John 3:16). Malls are usually full of people. God's Book reminds us that God loves each one of them.

15
Going to a Ball Game

LEARNING OPPORTUNITY

Whether it is big brother's midget football or major league baseball, most families spend some time as spectators at ball games. Even the most reluctant can use the opportunity to teach and to learn.

ACTIVITY STARTERS

1. Praise good sportsmanship when you observe it on either team. You might say, "I think God was pleased with the way that player handled that." Being a good example to our preschoolers when our favorite team is losing will help them begin to put their priorities in order.

2. If your team loses, tell your child that losing does not matter as long as the players did their best. Remind them that doing our best is all God asks of us. Ask your child to name opportunities when he has to do his best.

3. Think carefully about what you are saying to your child if you put a sporting event before service to the Lord. To do so is an ever-present temptation in our society. Saying, "I would really like to see the end of this game, but going to

church is more important," will make a lasting impression.

4. Allow your child to dress for the event. Let him wear team colors or, if he has one, a T-shirt or other piece of clothing with the name of his favorite (usually mom and dad's favorite) team. Help him make a banner to give support. Tell him, "I'm glad you are proud of the _____. We can be proud to be on Jesus' team, too."

5. Emphasize the importance of being together as a family. Tell your child you are glad to have his company. Make sure you have brought along items necessary for his physical comfort. Stadiums are not usually built with preschoolers in mind. Give thanks to God for allowing you to spend time together having fun.

A Bible Verse to Talk About

"Let us lay aside every weight, and the sin which doth so easily beset us, and let us run with patience the race that is set before us" (Hebrews 12:1). An athlete who is going to win must not let anything bother him while he is playing. God's Book teaches us that we must not let anything keep us from doing what God wants us to do.

16

Going to the Zoo

LEARNING OPPORTUNITY

Zoos provide an amazing assortment of God's creatures. A well-planned, leisurely trip can be a blessing to you as well as your child.

ACTIVITY STARTERS

1. Know something about the zoo you will be visiting, and be prepared. Children's zoos are usually smaller, with exhibits designed for the younger viewer. Large city zoos may require more than one trip for a young child—or at least a stroller. If you know nothing about a zoo, telephone and ask about size, layout (some have hills), and comfort accommodations. Tell your child, "Going to the zoo is God's present to us."
2. Prepare your child for your visit. You may not want to tell your child too far in advance that you are going to the zoo, but you can check out appropriate books from the library and begin reading them with him. Books about individual animals as well as about zoos will be helpful. Re-

read the Bible stories about creation and Noah and the ark.

3. Before leaving home on the day of your visit or while you are in the car, ask God to bless the time you will be spending together. You might pray something like, "Dear God, thank You for this day when we can be together. Help us to enjoy the animals You have created."

4. Help your child *look* at the animals. Ask him to describe them to you. Point out funny things you see them doing. Tell your child what the animal eats. Every now and then ask a question such as: "What kinds of problems do you think Noah might have had with an ＿＿＿＿＿＿＿ on the ark?" "If God had let you name the animals, what would you have called this one?"

5. Help your child tell about what he saw. At the dinner table (or picnic at the zoo) discuss the different animals. Give thanks for the animals God created. Ask the child to tell certain interested people (such as grandparents) about one animal that especially caught his interest. During the days that follow ask, "Why do you think God created ＿＿＿＿＿＿＿?"

A Bible Verse to Talk About

"For every beast of the forest is mine, and the cattle upon a thousand hills" (Psalm 50:10). God's Book says that all animals belong to God because He created them.

17

Going on a Trip

LEARNING OPPORTUNITY

Traveling with a preschooler can become a learning opportunity for the parents. Unless careful preparations are made, such trips can be a chore. However, with planning, trips by air, car, bus, or train can be pleasant and memorable.

ACTIVITY STARTERS

1. Prepare your preschooler for the trip. Explain that it will take a long time. "Five-and-a-half hours" means little to a three year old. If you will be traveling for more than a day you might say, "We will be riding in the car all day for one day, we will stop at a motel to sleep, then we will ride for part (or most) of the next day." Tell him some of the things God made that he might see along the way that are different from things he sees at home. If you are using a new means of travel, check the children's department of your library for books about trains, airplanes, or buses.
2. Pack a travel bag that includes different books (these can be from the library), a coloring book or unused pad of pa-

per, a new box of crayons, a small amount of modeling clay, sewing cards, small toys (but not small enough to be swallowed), treats, small drink cartons, sealed towelettes for clean-up, trash bags, and (if potty training) a coffee can for emergencies when there is no place to stop. This can is also useful in the case of motion sickness. The secret to the success of the travel bag is for the contents to remain a surprise until they are presented to the child at prudent intervals. You might say, "These are all things we need for traveling. God has given us all we need to know about how to live in one book—the Bible."

3. Plan stops along the way to break the monotony of the trip. A surprise picnic at a rest stop, a few minutes at a scenic view, or a brief visit to some attraction you are passing will serve as a change of pace. When you get back into the car you will have something new to talk about. You might say, "Can you tell me three things you saw that God made?" or, "How did looking at that mountain (river, valley) make you feel?" Treat any unexpected detours (or getting lost) as surprise side trips. Our family once saw a ship passing through a drawbridge, rode on a ferry, and discovered an interesting historic marker all in one afternoon of being lost. We have pictures of all three.

4. Sing songs or play games. Not only will these activities keep your child from becoming restless, but they will keep the driver awake. Some games may be modified. "I Spy" can be limited to items in the car. An older brother or sister can keep a list of state license plates, and a younger child can keep a list of the different colors of license plates. Bible questions asked by a parent are fun. The questions can be geared to the age and knowledge of each child.

5. Before you begin any trip, ask God's blessing upon it. My husband not only asks God to watch over us, but he also

prays that God will help us have a good time together. That is not a selfish prayer. Good times together are essential and build strength needed to face more difficult times that will come.

A BIBLE VERSE TO TALK ABOUT

"The Lord is my shepherd; I shall not want" (Psalm 23:1). A shepherd always watches over the sheep. God's Book tells us that we cannot go anywhere where God, our Shepherd, is not watching over us.

TEACHABLE MOMENTS IN NATURE

18

A Big Storm

The types of storms your family experiences will depend largely on where you live. Thunderstorms, tornadoes, hurricanes, and blizzards can all cause anxiety in children as well as adults. They can also create opportunities for talking about our beliefs and building relationships. My children miss the frequent retreats to our Indiana basement where we would wait out tornado warnings. Often friends without basements would often join us, making special memories.

ACTIVITY STARTERS

1. Plan ahead for the types of storms most likely to occur in your area. Keep basic requirements for riding out a storm on hand: light, heat, water, and food. Perhaps you and your child could work together to gather supplies. Include a Bible with the things you store. Say, "The Bible can help us when hard times in life come along, just as these other things can help us in a storm."
2. Help your child admire the beauty of the storm. Few things show the power of God's creation like a thunder-

storm. If you can view the lightning from a safe spot, cuddle and watch. The roar of a hard rain can be awe-inspiring. The swirling blankness of a blizzard is incomparable. Ask questions such as, "What does the wind sound like?" and, "What does the thunder remind you of?"

3. Take any fears to the Lord. Storms can pass from interesting to dangerous. If you see that your child is afraid, pray with him. Remind him of the time Jesus stopped a storm by speaking to it.

4. Read Bible stories by flashlight if the lights go off. Your child will probably be disappointed when the electricity returns.

5. Camp out. Once when my husband was away and a passing thunderstorm had taken out our electricity, my daughters and I spread sleeping bags on the living room floor and slept there. An inconvenience was turned into an adventure that created memories as well as security. When the electricity goes out you might assure your child with the statement, "Jesus can see in darkness as well as in the light."

A Bible Verse to Talk About

"The Lord hath his way in the whirlwind and in the storm" (Nahum 1:3). Storms are part of God's creation. God's Book reminds us that God has complete control of storms.

19

Seeing a Rainbow

LEARNING OPPORTUNITY

One fall evening after a brief shower, a double rainbow appeared in the eastern sky. Reflected by the blaze of the setting sun, it stretched from one horizon to the other, drawing people from their houses to stare in awe. The colors were brilliant. I forced myself to turn away and get into the car to retrieve my youngest daughter from cheerleading practice at a local park. Climbing into the car, she exclaimed, "Did you see it? We stopped everything and stood on the tables and just looked." God created rainbows to seal a promise. Many people who do not even know that are still drawn to rainbows. Use that natural attraction to teach about God.

ACTIVITY STARTERS

1. Because rainbows have a way of appearing when you don't have access to the family Bible, memorize Genesis 9:13-16. As your child is gazing at the beauty of the rainbow, you can recite the passage. As the beauty fades, help him review the story of Noah and the Flood. End by saying, "Like the Bible words I told you said, God put the first

rainbow in the sky to seal His promise that He would never flood the whole world at one time again."

2. As your child is looking at the rainbow, ask, "Do you know what a promise is?" After listening to his response, say, "God always keeps His promises. Once He made a promise to Noah. He promised Noah that He would never send another great Flood over the entire world again. To seal this promise God put the first rainbow in the sky. If God believes keeping His promise is important, do you think we should be careful to keep our promises?"

3. Use the rainbow to inspire a time of finger painting on your kitchen counter. (No finger paint on hand? Use instant pudding or non-mentholated shaving cream. Food coloring can be added if you desire.) As your child creates a rainbow, open your Bible to Genesis 9:13-16 and read it aloud.

4. After viewing the beauty of a rainbow, pray with your child, "Thank You, God, for the beauty You put into the world. Thank You for colors that make everything so pretty." Ask your child what his favorite color is. Spend a few minutes looking for that color in God's freshly washed creation.

5. For a few days after seeing a rainbow, conduct a rainbow search. Watch for swirls of color in puddles of water, on walls catching the evening sun through a pane of glass, or even in an oil drip. Buy or borrow a prism and allow your child to experiment with color. Put a sheet of paper on the refrigerator. Label it, "Thank You, God, for color." Let your child place colorful pictures here.

A BIBLE VERSE TO TALK ABOUT

"There was a rainbow round about the throne, in sight like unto an emerald" (Revelation 4:3). God mentions a rainbow both near the beginning and the end of His Book as a sign that He keeps His promises. Sometimes people break promises, but God never does.

20

Seeing Mountains

Many of the great events described to us in the Bible took place on a mountain. Mountains are a great visual interpretation of God's majesty and power. Visiting them is an opportunity to implant reverence in a child's heart.

ACTIVITY STARTERS

1. If you are driving up a mountain with your child for the first time, try to do so in stages. Many mountainous regions are dotted with rest stops, picnic areas, and scenic views. Stop frequently to admire the scenery. This will also allow your family to get used to a change in altitude. Providing gum or something to drink will help relieve pressure in the ears. Enjoy different views with your child. Comment on how strong God must be to make mountains. Point out other mountains in the distance. Holding your child's hand will make him feel secure as he enjoys this new experience.
2. Choose Bible stories about events that took place on mountains: Abraham's willingness to sacrifice Isaac, the giving

of the Ten Commandments, and the transfiguration. Read these aloud and let your child try to visualize the events.

3. Take along cardboard and glue. Encourage your child (or work as a family) to make a collage of things he finds on the mountain. Title it, "On the Mountain God Placed . . ."

4. Take advantage of any hiking trails available, keeping in mind your child's limited ability. Many wonders of God can be seen along these trails. Often the animals living nearby have less fear of humans than those in danger of being hunted. Walk slowly. Tell your child he will have a better chance of seeing a deer or other animal if he is quiet. Take time to look at what is around you. Pause to give thanks for things that seem special to your child.

5. Think about the hymns and choruses you know. How many of these talk about mountains or climbing? Singing these as a family while you are driving through the mountains or sitting around a campfire will make them more meaningful to all of you.

A BIBLE VERSE TO TALK ABOUT

"For ye shall go out with joy, and be led forth with peace: the mountains and hills shall break forth before you into singing, and all the trees of the field shall clap their hands" (Isaiah 55:12). God's Book says that the beautiful things He made will praise Him. If we will take the time to really look at these things, we will want to praise Him too.

21
Seeing the Ocean

How often the opportunity to see the ocean comes will depend upon where your family lives. The ocean may be as common as your own backyard or so rare that no one in your family has witnessed its testimony to God's creativeness. There may be greater danger in not appreciating its beauty when it is more common than when it is rare.

ACTIVITY STARTERS

1. Help your child experience the ocean with his senses. During an uncrowded time encourage him to listen for a few minutes and tell you what he heard. Do the same thing with sight. Have him describe the smell of the ocean. Find things for him to touch: sand, shells, seaweed, water. Let him touch the tip of his tongue to his finger if his hand has been in the water. Ask, "What do you taste?" Thank God together for the ocean and for the ability to see, hear, smell, taste, and touch.
2. Read Genesis 1:9-10 aloud. Ask, "What do you think happened when God said, 'Let the waters under the heaven

be gathered together unto one place'?" Then ask, "Why do you think God created oceans?"

3. Find books in the library about sea life under the category *water life*. Visit an aquarium. If you can find magazine pictures of sea life (old *National Geographic* magazines are good sources), let your child make a scrapbook. Type or print out Scripture references about the ocean or fish. Some of them include Genesis 1:10, 26; Psalm 24:2; 95:5; and John 21:10. Check a concordance for others.

4. Walk in the ocean together. Say something like, "Do you know that the same water that is rolling over our feet has probably rolled over the feet of children in other countries?" This concept will be difficult for him to understand, but he will probably be interested. Ask, "Does God know and love those children like He does you?" Your child may want to find out which countries are on the other side of this ocean. Encourage his interest and help him find out answers.

5. Is there a lighthouse nearby? If so, go for a look. If possible, get out of the car and spend some time there. See if you can take a tour; some are open to the public. Tell your child about the purpose of lighthouses—giving guidance and warning of danger. You might say, "Those of us who know about Jesus should act like lighthouses for people who do not know about Him. Can you think of ways we can do this?" If they cannot (it may be too abstract for a preschooler), say, "Maybe we can live like Jesus wants us to so others can see the right way to live. We can guide them to Jesus." When you get home let them build a lighthouse with blocks or draw one.

A Bible Verse to Talk About

"The voice of the Lord is upon the waters" (Psalm 29:3). God's Book tells us that God controls the water. I like to think the noise of the ocean is telling us about how powerful God is. Listen and see what you think it might be saying.

TEACHABLE MOMENTS DURING SEASONS

22
Spring

LEARNING OPPORTUNITY

Although spring comes in stages, there is usually a day (or an hour) when we sense that spring has arrived. If possible, help your child feel the change. Warn him that winter might return for a few brief visits, but enjoy this beginning together.

ACTIVITY STARTERS

1. Go for a walk even if you have to wear boots to trudge through the mud. Find the most natural setting possible (park or woods), and look for signs of new growth. Check tree limbs for buds, move old leaves and look for grass shoots, investigate birds building nests, and so on. Give thanks for the reminders of God's continuing creation as you discover them.
2. The first day the windows can be opened in the spring is an event in itself. Together remove the storm windows and clean them. Working together on that day can build special memories. Of course, like any job, removing storm windows is easier and requires less caution if you do not

ask your child to help, but the time of togetherness is worth the extra work. Use the time to talk about God's grace in providing cleansing from sin. You might say, "When I work hard to get something clean, I think about God sending Jesus to earth to die so sin could be cleaned from our lives."

3. Plant seeds with your child. I like to plant marigold seeds that the child can remove from the easily recognizable dead blossom of the previous year's plant. While holding the black slivers in your hand, ask, "Do these look like flowers?" When your child answers no, you can reply, "No, they don't, but I believe God can make marigolds grow from these seeds. He planned it, and He can make it happen."

4. Growing vegetables is a wonderful experience whether your garden is a country acre or a planter on a city patio. As you plant, review the story of creation with your child. Remind him that everyone who plants has faith in the plan God started when He created the world. Pray, "Thank You, God, for your plan that will allow this food to grow."

5. Bring spring to someone who cannot get out to enjoy it. A dish garden, planter, or cut flowers make lovely gifts for a shut-in. Planting a flower border with your child for an elderly neighbor or grandparent who can no longer do so is a gift that will provide joy for the entire growing season. Use the opportunity to discuss Jesus' command to love one another.

A BIBLE VERSE TO TALK ABOUT

"Thou sendest forth thy spirit, they are created: and thou renewest the face of the earth" (Psalm 104:30). God's Book tells us that every living thing depends on God's Spirit for life. Spring shows us how God can make things like trees seem new. God can do that with people's lives too.

23
Summer

Even if summer offers no break in your normal family schedule, it is a good time to change your pace and way of doing things. This effort is even more important for families not planning extended vacations.

ACTIVITY STARTERS

1. Work together to improve your outdoor space, whether it is an apartment balcony, a spacious country yard, or something in between. Let your child help you make it more enjoyable. Weeds can be pulled, new chair cushions can be made, planters can be filled and cared for. Use your work time to appreciate some things God created.
2. The longer days of summer make sunrises and sunsets farther away from the time many people will be going to or returning from work. Enjoy them together. Read Psalm 113:3 aloud as you watch the event. Sing a simple praise song with your child.
3. Do the unexpected. Keep a couple of sturdy cartons handy to transport a regular weeknight meal to a park. Crock-

pots travel well, and stoneware dishes are permissible. Serve breakfast on the patio, or wake your child up for an early morning walk. Pray, "Dear God, thank You for these special times together."

4. Plan mini-trips. Most of us are good tourists everywhere but at home. Take a good look at a map of your hometown and the surrounding countryside as if you were seeing it for the first time. Let each child choose one place he wants to visit. Our youngest daughter often reminds us that it was her idea that once saved a disappointing vacation. Collect souvenirs and take pictures as if you were traveling from far away. Make a display or scrapbook entitled "Nearby Blessings."

5. Plan a summer project. Buy a bird book or borrow one from the library and look up and keep a list of every new bird you see. Keep a weather calendar. Talk about ways in which summer weather is different from weather in other seasons. As you work on these projects, discuss God's hand in them. Say something like, "God blessed us with so many types of birds (or weather). I am glad He did not make only one kind."

A BIBLE VERSE TO TALK ABOUT

"Behold the fig tree, and all the trees; when they now shoot forth, ye see and know of your own selves that summer is now nigh at hand" (Luke 21:29-30). God's Book says that we know summer is near when the leaves on the trees come out. Days and seasons pass by quickly. Let's enjoy each day we have together and always remember to thank God for it.

24

Changing Leaves

LEARNING OPPORTUNITY

When your child notices that there is a change in the trees around him, begin these activities. We are often tempted to rush a teachable moment and then fail because the vital ingredient, the interest of the child, is missing.

ACTIVITY STARTERS

1. If you know a farm family, try to arrange to visit them for a few hours. If this is not possible, drive through farm country. Look for farmers working in the field. Talk about the fact that even the best farmers need God's rain and sun during the summer and a dry time during the harvest season to bring in a good crop. Drive by a grain elevator, and explain that the grain harvested by the farmers in the area is stored in the towers.

2. If you live in apple country, drive to an orchard and let your child help you harvest apples for your family's use. Say, "The cool weather God brings in the fall helps the apples ripen. It also causes the color changes you see in other growing things." Cut open an apple, and look at the

seeds. Explain that the seeds grow new apple trees. When you get home, allow your child to help you make applesauce. A simple way of doing this is to peel and slice apples, put them in a pan with a small amount of water, and cook until they are soft. Let your child mash them with a potato masher. Sugar and cinnamon may be added but are not necessary. At the supper table pray, "Thank You, Father, for the beauty, good smell, and good taste of apples."

3. Make a leaf collection. This might be a practical activity for city dwellers. Visit a park and collect beautiful leaves. Young children will not be particularly interested in the types of leaves. Together enjoy the different colors, shapes, and textures. When you get home, let your child make a fall wreath by gluing the leaves onto a cardboard circle. Their beauty will last longer than you might expect. Give thanks together for the many ways God made the world beautiful.

4. Decorate your home for the fall season. Hang Indian corn on the doors, bind cornstalks to light posts or porch supports, pile pumpkins by a doorway. Wreaths can be made by folding cornhusks and stringing them on strong wire bent in a circle. Cornucopia do not need to wait for Thanksgiving—neither do the traditional hymns of harvest. After decorating, sing hymns around the piano if you have one.

5. If you live on a farm, preparation of food supplies for the coming winter months will be a part of your child's daily life. If not, these preparations may be more subtle. Do you stock an emergency shelf or can purchased fruits and vegetables? Perhaps you buy large bags of bird feed. Whatever you do, let your child help. Whenever possible, point out animals doing the same types of things. Squirrels in the park or ants crawling on a porch railing are probably all storing food for the coming season. Point out that God

has given these animals the knowledge to do this. Read Proverbs 6:6-8 with your child.

A Bible Verse to Talk About

"While the earth remaineth, seedtime and harvest, and cold and heat, and summer and winter, and day and night shall not cease" (Genesis 8:22). God's Book says that the seasons will continue to arrive as long as the earth exists. The changes they bring remind us that God is in control.

25
First Snowfall

LEARNING OPPORTUNITY

The first snowfall of the season may slip up on you during the night or come during the middle of the day well predicted by the weathermen. In either case, it will be greeted with enthusiasm by young children. As adults, we need to stifle our negative, practical reaction and view this wonder through the eyes of a preschooler. If you live in a climate where snowflakes rarely appear, adapt some of the activities to a cold, rainy day.

ACTIVITY STARTERS

1. Plan a first snow breakfast. My daughters, who are well past the preschool age, still expect pancakes and hot chocolate on the first snowy morning of the year. In fact, the first snow of the past season arrived the day before my annual trip to the Amish bulk store where I purchase cocoa—much to their disappointment. You may not want to begin a pancake tradition, but decide on a warm breakfast you are sure your child will enjoy, and stash the in-

gredients away. Pray on that morning, "Thank You, Father, for the warmth of this food and the beauty of this day."

2. Build a snowman, play in the snow, or go sledding. You don't have to do this everyday, but at least once a year have a snow frolic with your children, even if you would rather sit by the fire and toast your toes. These happy memories will last longer and make a greater impact than the lessons that you teach. If you come across something in your yard that is not particularly attractive in its usual state, point out to your children how different and beautiful it looks under a blanket of snow. "God can take the things in our lives that are not beautiful and change them just the way the snow has changed this _____ ."

3. Have a winter picnic. Spread a blanket in front of the window with the best view or in front of the fireplace. We have a fireplace, but rarely invest in wood, so I fill it with candles. Serve finger foods and hot chocolate. Remind your children, "This special time we are having together is a gift from God. Let's thank Him for it." This is a good time for remembering other special family times.

4. Make your home cozy. You may want to do this earlier than the first snowfall. Let your child help you get out quilts and afghans to have handy for family members to wrap up in on cold winter evenings. Extra throw pillows might make your family sitting area more comfortable. (If you live in an area that has bad winter weather, you might want to show your child your preparations for a winter storm: extra food supplies, bottled water, flashlights and batteries, fuel.) Pray together, "Thank You, God, for our warm home."

5. Do something for someone else. Shut-ins often view the first snowfall as the beginning of a long, lonely season. Bake a plate of cookies with your child's help and take it over. Cold weather is not welcomed by the street people

of our cities. Gather up extra blankets, spare coats, or warm sweaters to donate to a mission. Say, "God has blessed us, and He wants us to share our happiness."

A BIBLE VERSE TO TALK ABOUT

"Thou hast set all the borders of the earth: thou hast made summer and winter" (Psalm 74:17). Have you ever noticed how often you feel ready for a change of season when it arrives? God's Book says the seasons were created by God.

TEACHABLE MOMENTS DURING HOLIDAYS AND CELEBRATIONS

26
Easter

Ideally, the days from Palm Sunday through the following Saturday should be quiet, reflective ones, followed by a joyous celebration of Easter. We all know, however, that the week before Easter is often filled with bunnies and egg hunts. We need to find ways for these seeming contradictions to be used to teach Easter's true meaning.

ACTIVITY STARTERS

1. Work with your child to make a chart, graph, or banner to track the events of Holy Week. Use the following list of events, and add a drawing or symbol each day.

>   Sunday: Triumphal entry (Luke 19:29-40)
>   Monday: Cleansing of the Temple (Luke 19:45-46)
>   Tuesday: Jesus answers many questions (Luke 20:1-8)
> Wednesday: Jesus is anointed with oil (Mark 14:3-9)
>   Thursday: Last Supper and/or Garden of Gethsemane
>   (Luke 22:19-20, 39-42)
>   Friday: Jesus dies on cross (Luke 23:32-33)
>   Saturday: Jesus is in tomb (Luke 23:53-56)
>   Sunday: Jesus rises from the dead (Luke 24)

2. Take advantage of warmer weather during the week, and go for a looking walk. Point out signs of new life to your child. You might say, "This Sunday will be Easter. We will celebrate Jesus coming back to life and the new life He will give us in heaven someday."

3. When you come across a worldly observance of Easter, remind your child that we already know that Jesus rose from the dead and these happy things are to help us express joy. Seek out such things as petting zoos in malls, and enjoy them with your child.

4. Include hot-cross buns in your holiday baking. Many recipe books contain instructions for making them, or you can use refrigerator sweet rolls and apply the icing in a cross. Preschoolers will enjoy helping. Use the working and eating time to bring out thoughts and conversation about Jesus.

5. Attend a sunrise service. Many families with young children unnecessarily deprive themselves of this beautiful experience. Missed sleep can be made up with afternoon naps. The early morning worship is often awe-inspiring for a young child and provides an opportunity for family worship.

A Bible Verse to Talk About

"He which raised up the Lord Jesus shall raise up us also by Jesus" (2 Corinthians 4:14). God's Book says that God the Father, who raised Jesus from the dead, will one day raise those who love Him from the dead. The resurrection of Jesus is so important that even mommies and daddies have trouble understanding it. Let's just be glad for it.

27

Mother's Day/Father's Day

These special days come around annually and can be great opportunities for learning to express love. Preschoolers may need a little help from the parent whose day it is *not* and acceptance from the parent whose day it is. Single parents should not feel self-serving in helping a preschooler celebrate the parent's special day.

Activity Starters

1. Help your child buy or make a gift for Mommy (or Daddy). As you do this talk about the ways that parent is a blessing to the child. Ask, "Do you think God is pleased when you show Mommy (or Daddy) how much you love her (him)? What are other ways you can show Mommy how much you love her?"

2. Be a good example in your expression of love for your own mother or dad. Never convey to your child that it is a chore. Let him participate in whatever you plan. Do not be embarrassed to let him hear you express love and appreciation to your parent. If your parent is no longer liv-

ing, tell your child what that parent meant to you. This could be done by saying, "When I was little my mom (or dad) taught me _____ about God."

3. Worship with your child. If he is usually in a children's worship, perhaps he would enjoy sitting with you in "big church" on your special day. Instruct him about what goes on in the adult services so he will feel comfortable and understand how he is to behave. Quietly compliment good behavior before, during, and after the service. "I think God was pleased with your behavior during worship this morning," will mean a lot if that compliment can be made honestly.

4. Plan a special family time during the afternoon. A walk, game time, or picnic will allow you to spend this day to its full potential. At some point during this together time, ask, "Why do you think God planned for people to live in families?"

5. During the week preceding, help your child make a poster entitled "Thank You, God, for a Mommy (or Daddy) Who Cares for Me." Let him search in magazines to illustrate the types of work or chores Mommy or Daddy does to earn money and help the family. Use the poster as the center of your decoration. During mealtime other family members can express why they are thankful for the honored one.

A Bible Verse to Talk About

"Honour thy father and mother; which is the first commandment with promise" (Ephesians 6:2). God's Book tells us that we should show love and respect to our parents every day.

28

The Fourth of July

LEARNING OPPORTUNITY

Citizenship, like Christianity, is best taught at home. Our nation's birthday is a good time to emphasize the duties and privileges of a Christian citizen.

ACTIVITY STARTERS

1. Attend parades, fireworks displays, or other events suitable for celebrating the Fourth of July. By your own example, teach your child to stand when the flag passes or is presented. Explain the meaning of various floats in the parade. Thank God together for allowing you to live in this country.

2. Even if you cannot leave your yard or if some family members have to work, make it a special day. Plan a birthday party complete with cake iced in red, white, and blue. String red, white, and blue balloons and crepe paper. A backyard picnic is better than no picnic at all. The same is true of an indoor picnic in case of rain. When the blessing is said, include thanksgiving for the freedoms we

have because we were blessed by being born in the United States.

3. Check your library before the holiday for picture books or easy-to-read books about the founding of our country or the celebration of the Fourth of July in earlier times. Read these with your child.

4. Before the holiday, teach your child a patriotic hymn. Take time to read the words and talk about what they mean. If you do not have a piano or keyboard, try to locate a record or tape that includes the hymn (check a library for records). Sing the hymn as part of your family celebration.

5. Make a patriotic mobile with your child. Cross and tie two twelve-inch dowel rods. Cut five stars or circles out of red poster board. Punch a hole in the top of each. Using string or yarn, tie each to the cross bar ends and center. Let your child find patriotic pictures that can be glued to the poster board pieces. Suspend the mobile in a prominent place. Use it to stimulate discussion about the blessings of freedom.

A Bible Verse to Talk About

"Submit yourselves to every ordinance of man for the Lord's sake" (1 Peter 2:13). God's Book tells us to obey the laws of our country. We should always be good citizens.

29
Halloween

LEARNING OPPORTUNITY

Many Christians have mixed emotions about Halloween. I am one of them. Halloween can exalt evil if allowed to do so. Since our children will be exposed to it to some degree, I feel we can use it as a time to teach good values, allow our children to have fun, and avoid glorifying evil.

ACTIVITY STARTERS

1. If the subject comes up, be honest with your children about the existence of evil practices such as witchcraft. (My family ran into some witches in a local fast-food restaurant a few weeks ago.) God does not teach against what does not exist. Assure them that those who love and serve God do not need to fear those who practice such things.
2. Encourage happy costumes. I have always felt strongly that my girls should not dress as witches, but we have had lots of fun with bunny, clown, kitten, pioneer, and Bible character costumes.

3. Use God's creations in your decorating. Pumpkins, corn-stalks, and Indian corn make beautiful decorations that usually last until Thanksgiving and provide opportunities for talking about God's blessings.
4. If you allow your child to go trick-or-treating, talk about the rules before you go. Encourage him to say thank-you to the people who provide the treats. Use the trick-or-treating time as together time. Walk along with your child, and help him enjoy God's creation of nighttime. On returning home, have a special family time. Popcorn and apple juice along with a few of his treats will make a special refreshment time. Before eating, give thanks for God's provision of food and safety.
5. Because of the dangers now involved with trick-or-treating, many schools and churches provide alternative activities. If nothing of that type is available in your community, perhaps you will want to have something on your own and invite a small group of your child's playmates. Simple games such as "Pin the Nose on the Pumpkin" could be played. Candy treats could be hidden around the room Easter-egg style (in a warm climate this could be done before sundown outside). Orange frosted cupcakes and apple juice would be appropriate refreshments. If your group is small, parents might enjoy coming also. You could end the evening quietly with a Bible story (an extra treat would be for some parents to act this out or present it as a puppet play). Use one showing courage such as David and Goliath, Daniel in the lion's den, or Caleb and Joshua. You might end by saying, "The person in our story was brave because God was with him. Part of the fun of Halloween is pretending to be scared, but we know we can always be brave because God is with us."

A Bible Verse to Talk About

"My God is the rock of my refuge" (Psalm 94:22). Everyone feels afraid at times. When we do feel afraid we can know that God's Book tells us that God is able to protect us from anything that frightens us.

30
Thanksgiving

LEARNING OPPORTUNITY

Every year Thanksgiving becomes a little more lost among the early Christmas decorations. The contrast of this quieter holiday can, however, make it special.

ACTIVITY STARTERS

1. Worship as a family. If your local congregation does not have a Thanksgiving eve or Thanksgiving Day worship service, attend a community service. Being thankful is one subject that can unite us all. If your child is not usually in adult worship services on Sunday, take time before you leave home to explain what will be happening and what type of behavior you expect from him. You might give him two or three things to look or listen for. Try to sit where he can see what is going on around him.

2. Make a Thanksgiving banner together. A half yard of fall-colored felt or burlap and some scraps of contrasting colors plus a little glue are all the materials you need to make a meaningful reminder of Thanksgiving. Older children can help in designing and cutting. Little ones love to

glue. Do not worry about perfection. Those lopsided sheaves will become precious to you in coming years. Use the work time to talk about blessings your family has received during the past year.

3. Give everyone who would like to an opportunity to help prepare the Thanksgiving Day feast. Many things can be done ahead of time so Mom does not have to have everyone in the kitchen during the last hour while trying to get everything to the table at once. Vegetables can be cleaned the day before. Pies can be baked and stored. As you begin working with your child, pray, "Dear God, thank You for this food we have to work with. Help us to prepare it carefully and not waste Your gifts."

4. When mealtime arrives, give everyone an opportunity to express thanks. Before attacking the pile of food, allow each person to name at least one thing for which he is especially thankful.

5. Find ways of giving to others. Allow your child to participate in a community, church, or family project of giving to the needy. For example, if your church collects food to be distributed at Thanksgiving time, let your child help select what to take and carry it in. Say, "Sometimes people go through hard times such as sickness when there is not enough money for food. When that happens, God expects those of us who have plenty to give to those who do not have enough."

A Bible Verse to Talk About

"Sing unto the Lord with thanksgiving; sing praise upon the harp unto our God" (Psalm 147:7). True thanksgiving is not a day or a tradition but a state of mind. God's Book encourages us to take time to praise and thank the Lord.

31

Cutting or Buying the Family Christmas Tree

Learning Opportunity

Finding the family Christmas tree can be a wonderful time of togetherness and learning. Whether you cut your tree out of Grandpa's woods or buy it at the local tree lot, a little planning can make the event more meaningful.

Activity Starters

1. Set a time to go as a family to get the tree. Mark it on the calendar. Help your child anticipate the event by talking about it as a special time together. Your child will feel special because you believe it is important to spend this time with him.
2. At a meal before the event, discuss Christmas trees. Decide on the type and size tree you want. Ask, "Why do you think we use an evergreen tree as a Christmas tree?" Let the your child answer, then reply, "Most trees are not as pretty in the winter as they are in the summer. Evergreen trees look pretty all year long. They remind us that Jesus

came to earth so that someday we can live forever with Him in heaven." Read John 3:16 together.

3. Take time to enjoy the smell and feel of the trees on the lot or in the woods. Show your child how sticky the base of a freshly cut tree is. If you are in a wooded area, look for signs of wildlife. Don't let finding the "perfect" tree become more important than having an enjoyable time together. Unhappy memories will mar a perfect tree. Remember that proper placement and decorations will make even a lopsided tree beautiful. When you have found your tree, pray, "Dear God, thank You for this beautiful tree. Thank You for Jesus whose birth we celebrate with it."

4. Sing Christmas carols. If you are buying your tree from a lot, you may not want to sing there (most of us are a little shy about singing in public, and if you have older children it will embarrass them), but you can sing in the car going and coming. Your preschooler will not worry about your voice but will love to have you sing with him.

5. Care for your tree when you get home. If you are not going to put your tree up right away, be sure to saw a little off the trunk and place the tree in water. Tell your child, "God has given us many beautiful gifts like this tree, and we should always be careful to care for them in the right way." You may want to make your child responsible for watering the tree each day after it is set up.

A BIBLE VERSE TO TALK ABOUT

"Out of the ground made the Lord God to grow every tree that is pleasant to the sight, and good for food; the tree of life also in the midst of the garden, and the tree of knowledge of good and evil" (Genesis 2:9). God's Book tells us that trees were created by God to be a blessing to us. It seems appropriate that this gift be used in celebration of His greatest gift, His Son, Jesus.

32

Family Birthdays

Learning Opportunity

A preschooler's own birthday looms before him with the promise of gifts and exciting possibilities. Gently guiding him to be generous during his own birthday and happy about the birthdays of others is a challenge for any parent.

Activity Starters

1. Have your child be involved in the planning of his own special day, encouraging him to include others in his plans. Be honest about what he can expect. A child's party does not have to be expensive if you use your imagination. Most refreshments can be homemade. A theme is helpful. One of our most successful birthday parties used a puppet theme. The cake was made of layers cut into strips and circles that could be placed into the form of a marionette. The strings were made with extra icing. The biggest expense was a package of plain, white tube socks. These were transformed by the guests into hand puppets with bits of felt and yarn. The puppets became the entertainment as the guests were divided into teams to act out

stories. (Bible stories work well.) At the end of the party these same puppets became favors for each child to take home. During the planning of his party, remind your child to be thinking about what his guests will enjoy.

2. Include children in planning birthday surprises for others. You might say something like, "We are thankful God gave us _____. What can we do for his birthday to make him feel special?" A surprise party can be given for a family member with only the family present and still be a great success.

3. Help your child make gifts for family members or give him simple chores so that he can earn a little money to buy a gift. Giving will be more important to him if he has sacrificed something in the giving. Remind him of God's gift, Jesus, as he works. Scrapbooks, covered juice cans, bookmarks, and many other simple gifts can easily be made by preschoolers. Give their gifts dignity by wrapping them as carefully as you would an expensive gift.

4. Encourage family members to give secret gifts on another member's birthday. Finding chores done, a flower by one's bed, or a handmade card adds excitement to the day and requires little or no expense. Tell your child that Jesus is pleased when we are kind to each other.

5. Thank God for what the person celebrating a birthday means to your family. During the birthday celebration, have a time when each one tells one reason he is thankful for that person. Have a special prayer time asking God's blessings on and thanking Him for the one being honored.

A BIBLE VERSE TO TALK ABOUT

"Teach us to number our days, that we may apply our hearts unto wisdom" (Psalm 90:12). God's Book teaches us to spend our days wisely. A birthday is a good time to think about whether we are pleasing God every day. It is also a good time to plan ways to please Him more.

TEACHABLE MOMENTS IN NEW EXPERIENCES

33

The First Day of School

School experience is beginning earlier and earlier. Whether your child's school career starts in a three-year-old preschool or traditional kindergarten, his first day should be a positive one. You will want to convey the idea that this is an important, exciting step in the child's life and deal with any fears he may have about being separated from home or being in new surroundings.

ACTIVITY STARTERS

1. Help your child make a going-to-school collage. A couple of weeks before school begins, tape a length of paper to a wall. Print the words of Psalm 121:5, "The Lord is thy keeper," on the paper and tape a snapshot of the child's school under it. Provide glue, scissors, and any back-to-school circulars featuring school clothes or supplies that you find in the mail or newspapers. Encourage him to add to his collage. Pictures of pencils, lunch buckets, tape, and so on could also be glued on. Each day read the words on the collage and ask questions such as, "Do you

96

think God already knows where your classroom will be? Will God be able to watch over you at school? Will God know what you are doing at school and I am doing at home (or work) at the same time?"

2. Make shopping for school clothes an event. Be sure to take into consideration your child's tastes and current styles. Remember that peer pressure begins early. A little girl sent to school in ruffles and lace when all the other girls are wearing more casual clothing may be reluctant to return. Pray that you will be able to find appropriate clothes, and thank God for the money He has provided to buy them. Stopping for refreshments, if the family budget will allow, will add emphasis to this time and provide an opportunity for discussion. Say, "You are starting to grow up and have new things happen in your life. I hope you will always ask God what you should do when it is time to try new things."

3. Have a first-day-of-school party. Keep it simple in case it becomes a family tradition, as it has in our family. A cake (you can decorate it with gumdrops if you are not skilled in cake decorating), a pretty table setting, and small, wrapped gifts (pencils, figure erasers, and so on) are all you need to make the occasion special. Ask your child to tell about the events of his first day of school during dinner. Close with a prayer thanking God for your child's opportunity to go to school and prepare for doing God's work.

4. Establish a together time between at least one parent and each child every day. This will often be only a few minutes, but they are important minutes that can be lost when everyone is adjusting to new schedules and responsibilities. If possible, the first few minutes after a child comes home from school are best. They are filled with exciting news that may be forgotten after an hour or so at

home. If you drive your child to and from school, time in the car is often good for talking. Asking your child, "What did Jesus help you learn today?" as soon as you get home will establish a time for your child to talk to you. If at all possible, sit down while he talks. If there are problems, take time to pray with your child and make notes to remind you to follow up on those problems.

5. Make your interest known to your child's school staff from the first day on. Volunteer to do whatever you can. Attend all teacher conferences. Let teachers know if any problems arise at home that may influence your child's emotions. Accept your child's teacher as a teammate in guiding your child, and pray for her. Encourage your child to thank God for his teacher, for books, and for being able to go to school.

A Bible Verse to Talk About

"Behold, I am with thee, and will keep thee in all places whither thou goest" (Genesis 28:15). God's Book tells about a promise God made to Jacob as he left home, promising him that He would be with him. We need to remember that there is nothing God cannot do and nowhere He cannot be.

34

First Overnighter

LEARNING OPPORTUNITY

Allowing your child to sleep over at a friend's house or having a friend sleep over at your house is a milestone in growing up. Lessons learned may be planned or unplanned, pleasant or not so pleasant.

ACTIVITY STARTERS

1. If the event is taking place in your home, keep family routine in place as much as possible. Casually fit the guest into your family instead of rearranging your family around the guest. Everyone will feel more comfortable, and seeing what your home is really like will be a learning experience for the visiting child. If he is from a non-Christian family, this visit could be his first exposure to Christianity.

2. If your guest is very young, be prepared for him to change his mind and decide to go home. Warn your child before the guest arrives that this might happen. If it does, assure the visiting child that you really would like for him to stay but that you will not force him to do so. After the

departure, comfort your child and tell him that in a few months his friend may feel ready to try another visit. This would be a good time to talk about David and Jonathan's friendship (1 Samuel 20:18-42). Tell your child that one time Jonathan had to tell David to go away so he would be safe. Remind him that he had to let his friend leave so he would be happy.

3. If the guest appears to be settled for the night, but the children's enjoyment of one another is growing thin, feel free to step in. Quiet activities such as having a story read, listening to a tape, or looking at family pictures are diverting and relaxing. Compliment them on playing well together before trouble begins. You might say, "God likes to see people getting along well together."

4. Plan a celebration breakfast. Place berries or chocolate chips on pancakes to make happy faces, or make pancake men. Bring Proverbs 17:17 on a folded index card and put it on the table. Tell the children that it says "A friend loveth at all times" and that you are happy they are friends.

5. If your child is to be the guest, prepare him as well as his overnight bag. Tell him where you will be and what you will be doing. Unless you will be out of town (a trial run would be better before such a visit), assure your child, if he asks, that he can always come home. Remind him, "God will be watching over you at Brian's house just as He does when you are at home."

A BIBLE VERSE TO TALK ABOUT

"The Lord is thy keeper" (Psalm 121:5). God's Book tells us that God watches over us and protects us. God watches over you even when we are not together.

35

Moving to a New Town

A move to a faraway place is often easier for very young children than for older preschoolers or school-age children, because the younger the child the more his life centers around his family. Even a baby, however, can be upset by a move if he senses emotional stress in family members. Use this time of separation from familiar people and places as a time to draw closer as a family and to God.

ACTIVITY STARTERS

1. As a family, memorize Hebrews 13:8. Recite it when someone mentions something being different. You might say, "Our lives seem different now, but we know, 'Jesus Christ [is] the same yesterday, and to day, and for ever,' and that makes us able to stand change."
2. Find a new church quickly. Ask the minister in your old church to help you locate a congregation that is most likely to fit your needs. This is not a time to visit around for six months. You and your children need the security of Christian friends. Do not expect the new church to be

just like the old one. You will never find another one like it. Unless there is something about the church and its teachings you feel are contrary to God's Word, settle in quickly and get busy. Go to Sunday school, join the choir, volunteer for nursery duty—anything to get involved. Comment on positive things. "Your Sunday school teacher seems friendly" is more comforting than "Did you like your new Sunday school teacher as well as Mrs. Smith at our old church?"

3. Become acquainted with your new community. After a basic unpacking of the necessities, the remainder can wait a bit. Take time to tour shopping places, parks, and other spots of interest. Go to the public library and sign everyone in the family up for a library card. If funds permit, join the local YMCA and enroll in a class or two. Look for positive things to comment on in front of the children. Give thanks for those positive things when you finish your tour.

4. Read together (beginning before the move) a book about a family from another time. Some of the *Little House* books are good for this. Covered wagons seem more exciting than moving vans and station wagons, but the same emotions can be shared.

5. Establish new together times or family traditions. If you have never had Bible reading (or Bible story reading) at a certain time, you might find it easier to establish now with the change in routine. Do it soon after the move, as habits are formed quickly. Listen carefully to the prayers of your children during these first few weeks. They may reveal needs that they do not express elsewhere.

A BIBLE VERSE TO TALK ABOUT

"The people answered him, We have heard out of the law that Christ abideth for ever: and how sayest thou, The Son of man must be lifted up? who is this Son of man?" (John 12:34). God's Book tells us about people in Jesus' day who were undergoing a lot of changes. If Jesus was really God, they wondered why was He talking about dying. But they did know that Christ was to live forever. Today we can be comforted by that same fact.

36

Arrival of a New Brother or Sister

LEARNING OPPORTUNITY

Birth order and a child's age have a lot to do with how he receives a new brother or sister. All new arrivals bring a change of routine for the entire family, and that can prove upsetting for a preschooler. Easing him into the experience may soften the changes and help him anticipate and accept the coming of a new family member.

ACTIVITY STARTERS

1. Make your preschooler aware of what is going to take place. You may not want to tell him as soon as you tell your husband, but he should be one of the first to know. Secret conversations are too often interpreted negatively by children. If you tell him your secret before you tell your friends, it will make him feel special. Speak of the new baby as a blessing from God. You might say, "When God sent you to our family, it was one of the best things that ever happened to us. I am sure this new baby will be a blessing to all of us too."

2. Let your child be part of the preparation team. Planning for and working on a place for the new baby will be exciting. As you set up different equipment, explain its use. If at all possible, do not use your preschooler's space for the baby, but if that is the only solution, try to lead him to make the suggestion. In either case include a few new touches for the older child's space as you shop. A new poster or two, some new curtains (from a garage sale if necessary), or a fresh coat of paint will keep him from feeling neglected. Talk about the preparations Mary must have made for baby Jesus.

3. When the new baby has arrived, encourage the older child to join both of you during quiet times. Encourage him to sing gently with you choruses and hymns that you both know. This is a wonderful time for Bible stories. You can tell them when your arms are busy and read them when your arms are free. Many experts say it is never too soon to begin reading to a child. I believe it is never too soon to expose him to God's Word.

4. Give your child a specific responsibility toward the baby. Perhaps he could be in charge of washing rattles and other washable toys. Tell him that perhaps one reason God made families was so we could care for one another. Talk about ways other family members care for each other.

5. Celebrate the expanded family. One of our best family memories is of a moment soon after Sandy was born when we were all sitting on the sofa and Kellie announced with joy, "All my peoples are here!" Enjoy times when all your "peoples" are together. Give thanks for them. Start a family blessings journal. When special times occur, ask your child, "Should we write this down?"

A BIBLE VERSE TO TALK ABOUT

"How good and how pleasant it is for brethren to dwell together in unity" (Psalm 133:1). God's Book says that God loves to see His children live together without fighting. To do that we need to love each other and care about each other's feelings.

37

Moving to a New Home

LEARNING OPPORTUNITY

Young children enjoy the security of familiar surroundings. Moving to a new house, even if it is in the same town or neighborhood, can be a unsettling experience if it is not thoughtfully dealt with by parents. A gradual, prayerful introduction and a thoughtful move can make this an adventure as well as a time of strengthening the family.

ACTIVITY STARTERS

1. Visit the new home, more than once if possible, before moving day. Let your child see where his special place will be. If more than one child will be sharing a room, together plan for bed placement and closet space. If you will be redecorating before the move, allow your child to participate in the details. Ask, "What are some of your favorite colors?" If the child chooses three or more, choose two and say, "Would you rather paint your room _____ or _____?" (This eliminates being stuck if your child says his favorite color is black!) Before leaving, pray, "Thank You, Father, for this

new place to live. Help us fill it with love and praise for You so it soon will feel like our home."

2. Before moving day, make a welcome kit for the people who will be moving into your old home. It could include a chart of the immediate neighborhood with neighbors names and telephone numbers, close and reliable baby-sitters, tips on good places to shop, and an invitation to visit your church. All of these will be especially helpful if the new people are moving from out of town. A brief note wishing them happiness will be appreciated. The children could each draw a picture of a happy time spent in the home. Add a Scripture reference card or an inspirational magnet. This welcome kit can be placed in a plastic, seal-able bag and put inside a kitchen cabinet. Pray for the new family.

3. Keep a spirit of adventure on moving day. Wake the children early and spend a few quiet moments with them before the movers descend upon you or the truck arrives and you have to begin loading boxes. During these quiet moments discuss what will be happening and any plans you may have made for them. Say something like, "When today is over we will have moved all of our things into the new home. Then we can begin to put your new room in order. We can put together your bed and unpack your toys. Won't that be fun? Let's ask for God's help today. 'Dear God, it is going to be a busy day. Please help us to be happy workers as we move to our new home.'" Even if your child will be staying with someone while most of the moving takes place, plan a few small jobs for him so he can feel a part of everything.

4. Let your children help pack a security bag on moving morning and place it in your car where you can get to it when needed. The younger your child the more impor-tant this is. Include changes of clothes, pajamas, tooth-

brushes and toothpaste, a couple of towels and washcloths, plus his special toy, blanket, night-light, or anything else that might be needed before the next day. Add a Bible to this bag to use in worship time.

5. Have a moving day worship time. Keep it simple, since even the best of moving days tend to be hectic. A special time of Bible reading and thanksgiving around the supper table (or packing box) or at bedtime is sufficient. The story of Abraham moving his family (Genesis 12:1-7) would be appropriate. Pray, "Dear God, please bless our new home. Help us to always honor You here by what we do and say."

A BIBLE VERSE TO TALK ABOUT

"The curse of the Lord is in the house of the wicked: but he blesseth the habitation of the just" (Proverbs 3:33). God's Book tells us that God blesses people who live good lives. One way to please God is to be thankful for our home and to be satisfied with changes.

38

Going to the Hospital

Children are often frightened by the unknown. That factor combined with the sickness or pain that usually accompany a hospital stay can be overwhelming. Since trips to the hospital can come about suddenly and unexpectedly, it is best to prepare for them when everyone is feeling well.

ACTIVITY STARTERS

1. Acquaint your child with the local hospital. Call to see if any tours are given. If not, conduct your own limited one. Drive around the hospital. Point out the emergency door and explain that ambulances bring sick and injured people there for quick help. Park and walk around the grounds. Show the children the windows of the patient rooms. Explain that they will not be allowed to visit those rooms because the people staying in them are not feeling well. Go into the lobby. Visit the gift shop, coffee shop, and chapel if it is off the lobby. Just this little bit of knowledge can help remove the strangeness of the hospital. When

you return to your car, give thanks for a place where sick and hurt people can go for help.

2. Purchase a child's doctor or nurse's kit, and encourage your child to care for his dolls or stuffed animals. Remind him to give them gentle, loving care. Play along with him, and teach him some truths as you do by saying something like, "This may hurt a little, Teddy, but just for a minute. It will help you get well." Tell your child that we should pray for doctors and nurses as well as the person who is sick.

3. Visit your local library and check out books about hospitals and health workers. Read these with your child and again give thanks for places and people that help people get well. Help your child send a thank-you card to his doctor and staff.

4. When your child or someone he loves must go to the hospital, remind him of what he has learned. Keep as much communication as possible going between home and hospital. Be honest with your child. Do not promise him that Grandpa will come home. Reassure him beforehand that God can care for Grandpa in heaven if he is too sick (or hurt) to live on earth anymore. Remind him daily of the loving care the sick person is receiving. If the child is the one in the hospital, encourage him to thank his nurses and doctors for helping him. Do not complain in front of him about what you believe is poor care.

5. Have a family project for a hospital or perhaps a Ronald McDonald House in your area. Find out about a needed item or service and provide it "in the name of Jesus" as a family. It might be something as small as a beautiful Bible storybook for the children's ward. Family members can save money to contribute toward the gift.

A BIBLE VERSE TO TALK ABOUT

"Thou compassest my path and my lying down, and art acquainted with all my ways" (Psalm 139:3). God's Book tells us that God knows about everything that is happening to us. He can take care of any situation.

TEACHABLE MOMENTS IN SADNESS

39

The Cat Disappears

Although this chapter title specifies a missing cat, it can be used for any pet. Cats just seem to have a better rate of reappearance. Whatever the pet, the uncertainty of not knowing is often more painful than its death would have been. We need to remember that time seems to move more slowly for a child than it does for us. They need to do something to try to find their pet.

Activity Starters

1. Spend time helping your child look for the pet. Walk or drive, using the time to talk about the pet. You may feel that the chances of finding your pet are all but non-existent, but you will be demonstrating your concern to your child. Pray that God will help you find your pet. When our oldest daughter's cat, Smokey, wandered away during his final illness, her greatest consolation came from hearing that her dad (who is not a "cat person") walked through fields in the rain looking for him.

2. Allow your child to advertise. Have him illustrate small posters. You can do the printing. These can be posted in local convenience stores or laundries. Remind your child as he works that even though he does not know where his kitty is, God knows and cares. Newspaper ads can also be helpful and well worth the expense.

3. Try to locate an article about the comfort animals can be to lonely, older people. Ask your child to think about all of the good things that could be happening to his pet. Allow him to get a little carried away in his imagination. Pray with your child, "Dear God, You know we love and miss _____, but we want him to be happy. Please care for him wherever he is."

4. After a sufficient amount of time has passed, bring things to a close with a time of remembering. Ask all of your immediate family to participate. (Older children may feel silly, but they may be grieving for the pet, too, and not be willing to show it.) Ask everyone to relate a happy memory about the pet. Read Matthew 10:29. Say, "_____ was created by God just like the sparrows, and the Bible tells us God knows and cares what happens to them." Offer a prayer of thanksgiving for the happiness the pet gave you while he lived with you.

5. Do not make any quick judgments about replacing the cat. He may come back even after your time of remembering. A stray may show up on your doorstep right after you have proclaimed, "We'll never have another cat." Then your child's "But, Mommy, someone else may be taking care of _____; shouldn't we take care of this kitty?" will bring real problems. Let your child's needs guide your decision. Some children need pets more than others. A different type of pet might be in order. Talk and pray about it.

A Bible Verse to Talk About

"A righteous man regardeth the life of his beast: but the tender mercies of the wicked are cruel" (Proverbs 12:10). God's Book teaches us that people who love God treat all living things kindly.

40

The Death of a Pet

LEARNING OPPORTUNITY

The death of a pet may affect different families or even family members in different ways. The way a pet dies—whether by accident, sickness, poisoning, or old age—can cause different feelings. The pet may have been a member of the household for as long as your child can remember. The death of a pet may be the first experience with death for many children.

ACTIVITY STARTERS

1. Allow your child to grieve, and offer comfort and sympathy. Crying with your child is more comforting than urging him to stop crying because the pet was "only an animal." The more unexpected the death, the more necessary this time of grieving becomes. A child who has known his pet was sick or very old may have done some grieving beforehand. Let your child know that God knows how he feels.
2. With proper attention given to sanitation, allow the child to help bury his pet if it died at home. A cardboard box

and a grave in the backyard are sufficient. Allowing the child (not forcing the child) to see the dead pet (unless injuries are too terrible) will help him accept the reality of the situation. You might use the opportunity to tell him how death was brought into the world.

3. Help your child say good-bye. Whether the pet was buried at home or his remains cared for by the veterinarian, a time of recognition of the death will help him release his emotions. A time of thanksgiving for the joy the pet has given is sufficient. Pray, "Thank You, God, for creating pets to enrich our lives. Thank You especially for _____ and the good times we spent with him." Answer any questions your child may have lovingly but truthfully. Do not make any promises God has not made. If a child asks, "Did my dog go to heaven?" You might answer, "The Bible only tells us that people have souls that live after they die on this earth. It does tell us that God cares about all the creatures He put on earth. _____ had a happy life here, and we know he is not in pain (or whatever is appropriate) any longer."

4. Let the child do something meaningful in his pet's memory. A bag of pet food delivered to the humane society will be more useful than something symbolic. Say, "God let us enjoy _____ for a long time. Now we can share some of the food we would have used for him with other animals."

5. Let your child's needs guide you in deciding about a new pet. Talk honestly with your child when he is ready to talk. Would another type of pet be better for your family? Would he rather wait until a pet finds him? They often do. Remind your child of the restrictions a pet puts on the family. Pray together, "Dear God, help us decide about a new pet."

A Bible Verse to Talk About

"For every beast of the forest is mine, and the cattle upon a thousand hills. I know all the fowls of the mountains: and the wild beasts of the field are mine" (Psalm 50:10-11). We often call our pets "my dog" or "my cat" and forget that God's Book tells us all animals belong to God. Although God wants us to enjoy their company, we should never become too possessive of them.

41

A Death in the Family

LEARNING OPPORTUNITY

Most of us assume that our child's first experience with death will be the death of a grandparent or other older relative. That is not always the case. Many very young children have to deal with the death of a playmate, sibling, or parent. Often we are not at our best at such a time to give our child the comfort he needs. We often have to ask God for an extra measure of strength, which He will provide.

ACTIVITY STARTERS

1. Do not shield your preschool child from the subject of death. We need to make our conversations about death or impending death a normal part of life so death will not be foreign to him when he is faced with it. There are some good books for preschoolers that deal with death. Check your Christian bookstore. You may find some in your public library also, but you will want to read these carefully before reading them to your child.
2. Be honest about your own grief, and encourage your child to express his, but do not be surprised if he does not. Of-

ten children react to death in ways adults do not understand. They may act as if nothing has happened. They may soon be bragging about it as a ploy for attention. In fact, a child's grief reaction may not set in until months after the death of a loved one. Perhaps that is God's plan to enable a parent and a child to minister to each other when each is hurting most. Reassure your child that God makes each person different and that the way he feels and reacts does not have to be just like other people.

3. As a family, spend more time reading God's Word, praying, and worshiping. Your example will point your child to the Source of help. Tell your child, "I feel a need to spend more time with God right now while I am feeling so sad. He helps me feel better." Do not stay away from church because you are afraid of crying in public. Your brothers and sisters there will understand.

4. Spend time with your child recalling happy times (even funny times) spent with the one who has died. Look at family pictures. This could easily lead to a discussion about how happy the loved one is now. You might want to ask, "What do you think _____ is seeing now? How do you think God is caring for _____?"

5. After the death of a loved one, notify all adults who will be dealing with your child. A Sunday school teacher, schoolteacher, or day-care worker will be better equipped to correctly interpret any change in behavior and to deal with them if you do so. A brief note is all that is needed.

A BIBLE VERSE TO TALK ABOUT

"For we have not an high priest which cannot be touched with the feeling of our infirmities; but was in all points tempted like as we are, yet without sin" (Hebrews 4:15). God's Book tells us that Jesus understands how we feel.